914.31
Hoov

DATE DUE

APR 1 0 1985

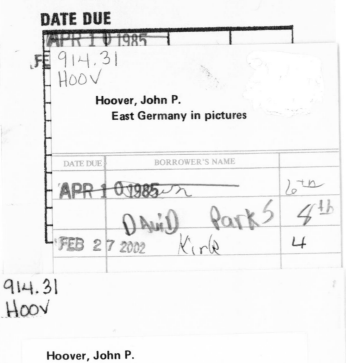

914.31
Hoov

Hoover, John P.
East Germany in pictures

DATE DUE	BORROWER'S NAME	
APR 1 0 1985		6th
	DAViD ParkS	4th
FEB 2 7 2002	Kirk	4

914.31
Hoov

Hoover, John P.
East Germany in pictures

EAST GERMANY
in pictures

Goethe founded this elegant library at Weimar.

VISUAL
GEOGRAPHY
SERIES

By **JOHN P. HOOVER**

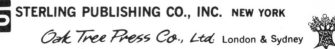 STERLING PUBLISHING CO., INC. NEW YORK

Oak Tree Press Co., Ltd. London & Sydney

VISUAL GEOGRAPHY SERIES

Afghanistan
Alaska
Argentina
Australia
Austria
Belgium and
  Luxembourg
Berlin
Bolivia
Brazil
Bulgaria
Canada
The Caribbean
Ceylon
  (Sri Lanka)
Chile
China
Colombia
Costa Rica
Cuba
Czechoslovakia
Denmark

Dominican
  Republic
East Germany
Ecuador
Egypt
El Salvador
England
Ethiopia
Fiji
Finland
France
Ghana
Greece
Greenland
Guatemala
Guyana
Haiti
Hawaii
Holland
Honduras
Hong Kong
Hungary

Iceland
India
Indonesia
Iran
Iraq
Ireland
Islands of the
  Mediterranean
Israel
Italy
Ivory Coast
Jamaica
Japan
Jordan
Kenya
Korea
Kuwait
Lebanon
Liberia
Madagascar:
  The Malagasy Republic
Malawi

Malaysia and
  Singapore
Mexico
Morocco
Nepal, Bhutan
  & Sikkim
New Zealand
Nicaragua
Nigeria
Norway
Pakistan
Panama and the
  Canal Zone
Paraguay
Peru
The Philippines
Poland
Portugal
Puerto Rico
Rhodesia
Rumania
Russia

Saudi Arabia
Scotland
Senegal
South Africa
Spain
The Sudan
Surinam
Sweden
Switzerland
Tahiti and the
  French Islands
  of the Pacific
Taiwan
Tanzania
Thailand
Tunisia
Turkey
U.S.A.
Uruguay
Venezuela
Wales
West Germany
Yugoslavia

This new kindergarten serves a recently completed residential area in Karl-Marx-Stadt.

PICTURE CREDITS

The author and publisher wish to thank Panorama DDR, Berlin, for the photographs used in this book.

Copyright © 1977 by Sterling Publishing Co., Inc.
Two Park Avenue, New York, N.Y. 10016
Distributed in Australia and New Zealand by Oak Tree Press Co., Ltd.,
P.O. Box J34, Brickfield Hill, Sydney 2000, N.S.W.
Distributed in the United Kingdom and elsewhere in the British Commonwealth
by Ward Lock Ltd., 116 Baker Street, London W 1
Manufactured in the United States of America
All rights reserved
Library of Congress Catalog Card No.: 77-79502
Sterling ISBN 0-8069-1216-2 Trade   Oak Tree 7061-2561-4
1217-0 Library

Three happy medalists in diving competition are plainly proud of their accomplishments.

CONTENTS

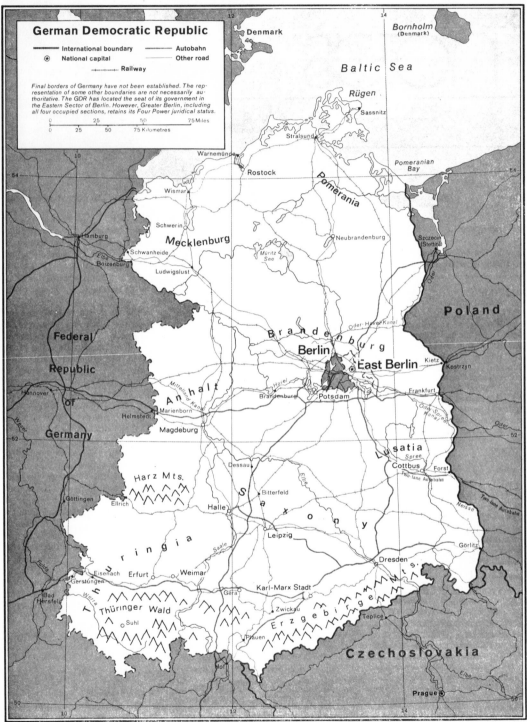

German Democratic Republic

—————— International boundary   —————— Autobahn

⊛   National capital   —————— Other road

+–+–+–+– Railway

Final borders of Germany have not been established. The representation of some other boundaries are not necessarily authoritative. The GDR has located the seat of its government in the Eastern Sector of Berlin. However, Greater Berlin, including all four occupied sections, retains its Four Power juridical status.

0   25   50   75 Miles

0   25   50   75 Kilometres

Denmark

Bornholm
(Denmark)

Baltic Sea

Rügen

Sassnitz

Stralsund

Warnemünde

Pomeranian
Bay

54

Rostock

Pomerania

Wismar

Schwerin

Mecklenburg

Neubrandenburg

Szczecin
(Stettin)

Hamburg

Schwanheide

Elbe
Boizenburg

Müritz
See

Ludwigslust

Oder

Poland

Federal

Oder-Havel Kanal

Brandenburg

Republic

Berlin

East Berlin

Kietz

Kostrzyn

of

Hannover

Mittelland Kanal

Anhalt

Havel

Brandenburg

Potsdam

Frankfurt

Oder-Spree Kanal

Germany

Marienborn

Helmstedt

Magdeburg

52

Oder

52

Dessau

Lusatia

Spree

Göttingen

Harz Mts.

Cottbus

Forst

Ellrich

Saxony

Bitterfeld

Two-lane Autobahn

Halle

Neisse

Two-lane Autobahn

Leipzig

Thuringia

Saale

Görlitz

Dresden

Eisenach

Erfurt

Weimar

Karl-Marx Stadt

Gera

Gerstungen

Bad
Hersfeld

Fulda

Werra

Thüringer Wald

Zwickau

Erzgebirge Mts.

Teplice

Suhl

Plauen

Hof

Czechoslovakia

Elbe

Prague ⊛

50

50

517547—3-75

Berlin is famed for the Unter den Linden boulevard, now lined with modern street lamps.

INTRODUCTION

The televised successes of East German athletes in the 1976 Olympic Games brought the German Democratic Republic (GDR) into the consciousness of the West. Ignorance compounded by Cold War attitudes assured that whatever information filtered through to the West was likely to be distorted to serve the requirements of ideological conflict. The truth, as it is beginning to be known in an era of détente, is agreeable and refreshing.

Though heir to a long tradition, the GDR has a short history. Born only a generation ago, it had a most inauspicious start. Its cities were bomb-blackened ruins, its factories tangled heaps of wrecked machinery, its rail and road transportation system a shambles, its seaports scenes of havoc, and its fields barren and weed-choked for want of farmers. Normal trade had given place to a nationwide black market; public services had broken down; hundreds of thousands of its men were prisoners of war; and a foreign army of occupation stood upon its soil.

In 1949, the GDR was formed as part of the post-war partition of Germany. Since then, after fitful beginnings, the truncated country has prospered. Its people have a sense of national identity, and the once war-shattered land has become a showcase of development, productivity, and social justice. As time passes, political and cultural indoctrination continues, the already pervasive economic and military integration into the socialist world proceeds, and the new feeling of separate nationality bids to become permanent.

In Halle District, the battlements of the Bernburg Castle grimly overlooked the Saale River in feudal times. They are anything but grim today.

This sail-flecked lake and its campground, near Karl-Marx-Stadt, are seldom empty.

The Brandenburg Gate, once a major symbol of the capital of the German Empire, now divides the two Berlins.

I. THE LAND

THE GERMAN DEMOCRATIC Republic (East Germany) or the GDR as it is known popularly, is bounded on the north by the Baltic Sea, on the east by Poland, on the south by Czechoslovakia, and on the west by a long frontier with the Federal Republic of Germany (West Germany).

Largely without natural frontiers and poor in natural resources, the German Democratic Republic is a remnant of a once-dominant Prussia, cut off from the huge, rich territorial base that supported the great military machines of World Wars I and II, when Germany stretched from the Low Countries on the west across Europe to Russia on the east. The Republic's boundaries are man-made lines,

drawn almost capriciously, by the victorious Allied statesmen at Potsdam, in 1945. Few areas are blessed with fertile soils; but an equable climate, adequate rainfall, and the absence of pronounced elevations permit the entire area to be used to advantage.

The area of the Republic is about 41,000 square miles (107,700 sq km)—roughly equal in size to Virginia or to all of Ireland plus Wales. The land can be divided into a coastal area, extending inland from the Baltic; central lowlands, not clearly separated from the coastal strip; and southern uplands, which likewise lack clearly defined boundaries, the transition from the lowlands being gradual.

Fishing and pleasure boats line the Old Stream at the seashore resort of Warnemünde.

THE COASTAL STRIP

Stretching east and west and extending from 15 to 50 miles (24 to 80 km) inland, this northern belt of land along the deeply indented Baltic coast is so dominated and influenced by the sea that it is considered separate and distinct from the rest of the broad North German plain. Of its four important offshore islands, the largest and most developed is Rügen.

The coastal lands are flat and low, with a few gentle hills, and cliffs along the coast. Otherwise, a monotonous landscape is relieved by many lakes and occasional marshes. Sandy soils predominate, in some places mixed with clays of varying densities. While not naturally highly productive, the land is made to produce rye and potatoes as main crops, with some wheat, sugar beets and maize.

Near Rostock is Fischland Beach, a summer resort on the Baltic.

Elbe River transportation is important to Magdeburg, a crossroads for rail, road and river traffic.

THE CENTRAL LOWLANDS

Between the northern coastal strip and the southern uplands lies a broad plain, where Berlin, the capital, and 8 surrounding counties account for most of the population, agricultural production and industry of the GDR. The mostly rolling land is dotted with lakes and covered with broad expanses of both deciduous and coniferous forests. Dark green pine forests, marbled with the white trunks of birches, make

Benches on the banks of the Spree River offer a comfortable resting spot for Berliners on an autumn afternoon.

From this comfortable and spacious observation tower, lifeguards keep close watch over swimmers at this lakeside resort in the Cottbus District.

New-fallen snow transforms the mountain town of Klingenthal-Muhlleiten, which is delightful during the summer, into a winter wonderland.

an agreeable sight. In general, the land slopes gently up from the coast, and is drained by important waterways including the Elbe, the Oder, the Spree and the Saale. Except along the rivers, soils are poor. While most of the area is devoted to mechanized and scientific farming, metalworking and other industries far outstrip agriculture in economic importance. Leipzig, the country's second city in population, and the important cities of Magdeburg and Halle are situated in this region.

THE SOUTHERN UPLANDS

The southern uplands extend across the country, uniting eastern Germany with both western and eastern Europe. They are an extension of the low mountain range that begins in southern Belgium, continues across both Germanies into Czechoslovakia and Poland, and ends as the Carpathian Mountains of Romania. In the GDR, the uplands are broken up into several areas. In the west, the mostly mountainous Erfurt District includes the wooded southern slopes of the Harz Mountains and the fertile Thüringer Basin. Immediately

Vacationers and tourists are drawn to Wernigerode, a picturesque summer resort in the Harz Mountains.

Quaintly uniformed musicians play traditional instruments on a crag high in the Erzgebirge Mountains.

to the south, the Thüringer Wald Mountains and forests of Suhl District are heavily populated with vacationers during the summer. To the east, the well-watered Gera District has forested hills and mountains and several of the country's largest dams and hydro-electric projects. Karl-Marx-Stadt (formerly Chemnitz) has most of the Erzgebirge Mountains and foothills, including the highest elevation, 4,770 feet (1,214 metres). Dresden District, like

A family enjoys a ski outing on the Fichtelberg peak, the GDR's highest, in Karl-Marx-Stadt District.

A managed forest is sprayed by helicopter. Such care eventually leads to more abundant yields of timber.

Tourists on Bastei Rock, near Dresden, have an eagle's eye view of traffic on the curving Elbe River.

Erfurt, combines mountains with several ranges of hills and, in the north, with plains.

The Harz area, the Thüringer Wald, in the southwest, and Erzgebirge, along the Czechoslovakian border, are the most densely populated and heavily industrialized regions of the southern uplands.

RIVERS

The GDR is drained by many rivers, the most important of which are the Elbe and the Oder. The Oder and Neisse Rivers are part of the eastern frontier with Poland, but drain only a narrow strip of GDR lands. The Elbe, the most important river, rises in Czechoslovakia, flows across the middle of the GDR, forms part of the boundary with the Federal Republic and reaches the North Sea near Hamburg. The Elbe drains virtually all of the central lowlands and southern uplands, and has four economically valuable tributaries. The first of these, the Havel, rises northwest of Berlin, flows through the western part of that city before joining the Elbe in Magdeburg District. From the Czechoslovakian border, the Spree flows north, cuts through the heart of Berlin and flows into the Havel. The Elde, from a source northwest of Berlin, drains Schwerin District before its confluence with the Elbe. The Saale, which rises in the Federal Republic, flows through Halle District on its way to the Elbe.

The Werra River, in the extreme southwest, has its source in the Thuringian Forest (Thüringer Wald), crosses Erfurt District, and enters the Federal Republic, where it unites with the Weser River. In the north, the short Warnow, Recknitz and Peene Rivers cross the coastal strip to flow into the Baltic.

Many of the rivers are important to internal and international transportation. Not only are they navigable for long distances but are linked by an extensive canal system. For example, the Elbe, navigable over its entire 355-mile (575-km) course, is connected by canal with the Weser River in the Federal Republic. Via the

Kayaks and canoes crowd the Tollense-See, a lake in the Neubrandenburg District.

Oder-Havel Canal, it joins the Oder system on the Polish border, and reaches the Baltic by means of the Elde River and canal. Of the Elbe tributaries, 470 miles (760 km) are navigable. The GDR's canal system has 150 miles (250 km) that are navigable by vessels up to 1,000 dead-weight tons (900 tonnes), and another 80 miles (130 km) by vessels up to 750 tons (670 tonnes).

LAKES

Most of the GDR's lakes are small and shallow, formed in depressions of the central

The botanical gardens in the important city of Frankfurt-an-der-Oder on the frontier with Poland offer flowers and greenery to summer strollers.

Young skiers enjoy an outing in the Thüringer Forest.

CLIMATE

The GDR is affected by both the maritime climate of western Europe and the continental climate of the great Eurasian land mass. In general, there are no great extremes of temperature, the overall average being 40–50°F. (4.4–10°C.). The weather is influenced by both the maritime and continental weather systems. In the northwest, temperatures are relatively even and the growing season long. In the southeast, winters are longer and colder and summers hotter. Annual precipitation averages about 24 inches (60 cm), most of it coming during the summer growing season when it is needed most. The southern uplands have 30–35 inches (75–87 cm) annually, the west central lowlands about 20 inches (50 cm).

lowlands, and have little commercial importance. They are concentrated northwest of Berlin, and in a belt beginning west of the city and extending to the south and southeast. There is a smaller cluster northeast of Dresden, and other lakes in the coastal strip.

SOILS

Nearly half the soils are glacial outwash, heavy non-porous clays or overly porous sandy types, virtually none highly productive. In the northern strip, soils do not retain either moisture or nutrients and are classified among the poorest in the country. Soils are better in the central lowlands, where large areas produce good

During the warm summer months, people like to cool off beside the pool and fountains in front of the Linden-Corso restaurant in Berlin.

Lignite, a low-grade coal, is one of the GDR's few basic resources. Much of it is scooped out of this open-pit mine near Cottbus.

yields of wheat, barley, sugar beets and fodders. On other soils of only average fertility, rye and potatoes are produced. Poor soils around Berlin are given over to forests and pastures. The southern uplands are mostly below average in fertility; in the western part, only 15 per cent of the land is cultivated and, in the south, about 3 per cent. The rest is forested.

Scientific soil conservation and cultivation practices, widely applied since 1950, have improved soil qualities and increased crop yields. Since almost all of the lands are accessible, those that are level and good enough are cultivated, leaving about 27 per cent of the area in managed forests, in which native oaks and beeches are being replaced with faster growing pine, fir and spruce.

WILDLIFE

Surprising in a country so long settled, there are sizeable numbers of wild animals. Varieties of mammals common to northern Europe are found, among them weasels, hares, foxes and marmots. The wisent, or European bison, which nearly became extinct in this century, survives in a few zoos and parks.

The forests provide a habitat for large numbers of wild animals. Beavers are found in the Elbe Valley, and non-indigenous muskrats have spread along many streams. Deer abound in the deciduous forests; in the coniferous forests are martens and wildcats. Wild boars are hunted in the densely wooded lowlands.

Among the game birds are the great bustard (a large turkey-like bird), found on open plains, and the cock-of-the-wood, a large grouse, which lives in the pine forests.

NATURAL RESOURCES

Most of the mineral resources, mainly lignite (brown coal) and potash, occur in a band of territory across the south-central part of the country. The GDR is the world's largest producer and user of lignite, and has developed the technology of its use to a high degree. From lignite come coke, briquettes, tar, gasoline, lubricating oils, gas, and electric power. About 90 per cent of the electricity consumed in the country is produced from lignite. Production processes have been developed that permit lignite derivatives to be used in the production of iron and steel. Near the Baltic coast, natural gas and petroleum are produced in very small quantities.

Potash is mined in and to the north of the Harz Mountains. In the western part of the Erzgebirge Mountains are minor deposits of bituminous coal, and, in the Harz Mountains, small quantities of copper and iron. Other minerals produced in token amounts include zinc, tin, tungsten, antimony, nickel, pyrites and uranium. The production of clay, kaolin, chalk and calcium sulphate meets local requirements.

This is the new Berlin, with its television tower and its Alexanderplatz, as seen by the operator of a tall crane. The Stadt-Berlin Hotel is in the middle.

CITIES

BERLIN (EAST)

Among new buildings of contemporary design, the old Town Hall of Berlin raises a traditional tower.

East Berlin has a population of 1,090,000—half that of West Berlin. From heaps of blackened rubble, a brilliant new city of light and culture has arisen, designed, with its open areas, more for people than for motor vehicles. From the vast central Alexanderplatz, broad avenues radiate into the downtown and outlying commercial and residential areas, and into the suburbs beyond. While some bullet-pocked buildings still stand, much of the planned reconstruction has been completed, providing apartment homes for about half the population. Additional modular apartment buildings are being completed so rapidly that the government is confident of providing modern housing for all the people within a decade. Already, high-rise apartment buildings in park-like settings are a major feature of the urban landscape. Colored and ornamental panels on outer walls relieve what would otherwise be a dull and stark uniformity of appearance.

Characters from Grimm's Fairy-tales live on as fanciful fountains in Friedrichshain People's Park in Berlin, to the delight of old and young.

In the heart of the city, gleaming stores, hotels, and public buildings line the main thoroughfares. From the Alexanderplatz rises the symbol of the reborn city—the minaret-like TV Tower, whose needle-pointed top frequently pierces the clouds. Modernistic fountains attract attention, and the sound of splashing waters soothes urban spirits. Apart from simple neon signs giving the names of buildings and kinds of businesses, advertising signs are absent.

Squares and streets throng with animated people, who would be inconspicuous among their counterparts in San Francisco, London, Sydney or Toronto. Shop windows offer attractive displays of tempting merchandise, and buyers respond. Eating places, from snack-bars to elegant restaurants, are numerous.

Buildings of historic, cultural and traditional value have been preserved, rebuilt or pains-takingly restored, among them the Opera House, State Theatre, Concert Hall, Museum, the University and the principal churches. Outstanding among the new buildings is the People's Palace, a huge marble structure which houses a variety of cultural and entertainment facilities—art galleries, lecture halls, restaurants and pubs, as well as the meeting place of the

This colossal statue rises from the middle of the huge memorial to Soviet war-dead in Berlin. A visit to this massive shrine is a "must" for tourists.

The German State Opera in Berlin rarely fails to draw capacity houses, as it has been doing for a century or more.

People's Chamber. Flood-lit walls and thousands of electric lights give it the nighttime appearance of a fairyland. Day and night, its marble-floored and carpeted halls and moving stairways are full of people, young and old.

Public transportation is extensive—buses, streetcars and elevated railways serve all parts of the city and an intricate network of underground trains speeds people everywhere. On all, single fares are the equivalent of a few pennies. Taxis are also plentiful. While streets are not usually clogged with vehicles, pedestrians quickly discover that jaywalking is dangerous, and locating parking space in many parts of the city is often a problem. Most cars are small and of GDR or Soviet manufacture, with others from Czechoslovakia and Poland. Many of the numerous large tourist buses are made in Hungary, while most of the vans, lorries and trucks of all sizes and shapes are products of domestic factories.

Canals and river channels crisscross the city, carrying barge and excursion traffic within Berlin and connecting with national and European canal systems. Railways and superhighways fan out to domestic points and link with international highway and rail networks. From the new Schoenefeld Airport there is frequent air service to and from overseas as well as domestic and other European points.

In Berlin, travellers find the conveniences, comforts, shopping and entertainment opportunities that are expected in a sophisticated major capital. The city is a tourist Mecca for travellers from the Socialist world, mainly from the countries of eastern Europe, Soviet Union, southeast Asia and Cuba. Other tourists come from the Middle East, Africa, Italy, Spain, and Portugal.

The city covers a large area and has a surprisingly large amount of open space—parks, the new zoo, sports fields, even agricultural areas, and an extensive Soviet war memorial of overpowering proportions.

Besides being the political, administrative, educational and cultural capital, East Berlin produces about 6 per cent of the national industrial output, including electrical equipment, machinery, clothing, rubber products, and precision instruments.

This miniature train, a real steam choo-choo, delights children in a Leipzig park.

Johann Sebastian Bach is greatly revered in Leipzig, as this statue indicates.

LEIPZIG

This second city of the GDR, population approximately 573,000, is a major trade, cultural, and industrial hub. It is also one of the principal railway junctions of eastern Europe, and the largest in the GDR. Publishing is a major industry of the city.

Leipzig is renowned as the site of the annual trade fairs that have been held since the Middle Ages. In 1970, no fewer than 6,500 exhibitors from 55 countries, including the United States, displayed and sold an immense variety of wares.

Leipzig boasts the Karl Marx University (formerly the University of Leipzig), which has a full range of faculties. Apart from the university, the city has many valued cultural traditions. Johann Sebastian Bach died in Leipzig, where he was for a long time director of the St. Thomas Choir and the School of Music. The Gewandhaus Orchestra, founded by Felix Mendelssohn, who died in Leipzig, is renowned throughout Europe. Richard Wagner was born in Leipzig.

The Thüringer Hof, famous in Leipzig since the Middle Ages, stands near the equally famous St. Thomas' Church.

The classic façade of the Georgi Dimitroff Museum, one of the world's finest, symbolizes Leipzig's renown as a cultural capital.

All these associations mark it as a city of music. In recent times the city has once more become a major eductional and scientific capital.

Since 1945, the city has taken great pride in its revolutionary history, starting with Robert Blum, who was prominent in the movement of 1848, and carrying on with such later social reformers as August Bebel, Karl Liebknecht, Rosa Luxemburg and Clara Zetkin. During the Nazi period, it was a major point of anti-fascist resistance.

Among the traditional tourist attractions, besides the 13th-century St. Thomas' Church, where Bach worked, are the Auerbachs Keller, a restaurant famous in the Faust legend, the beautiful 16th-century Old Town Hall, the Byzantine Russian Church (a monument to the Russian soldiers killed at Novgorod during the Napoleonic wars), and the German Library, which it is said contains every item of German literature ever published.

Modern additions to the city include the Sachsenplatz, bordered by old merchant houses, modern apartment buildings, adorned by flower beds, strikingly beautiful fountains, and sculptures. Others are the Opera House, where outstanding musical and theatrical productions are almost always in performance, the 100,000-seat Central Stadium for gymnastics and sports, and the towering skyscraper nucleus of the new university complex.

Badly damaged during World War II, Leipzig has been rebuilt, with neither effort nor expense being spared in the repair and restoration of its historical and cultural landmarks. The principal industries are machinery, chemicals, glass, ceramics, drugs, paints, textiles, clothing and furs.

DRESDEN

After having been virtually levelled at the close of World War II, this third city (population 507,000) of the GDR is a jewel of unbelievable beauty. Dresden is again a city of palaces, churches, museums and art galleries. Traditional buildings have been restored, and wherever one looks are picture-postcard scenes, all structures of amazing architectural harmony one with the others. Only a handful of gutted buildings are still awaiting reconstruction. A notable exception is the Baroque Frauenkirche (Church of Our Lady), which will remain a blackened hulk as a reminder of the horrors of war.

The Zwinger, or palace compound of the kings of Saxony, a complex of lovely Baroque buildings, is the major magnet for tourists. The royal art gallery offers a great collection of Old Masters—Rembrandt, Raphael, Titian and others—and modern greats, including Cézanne, Monet, Gauguin and Picasso. In addition, there are a large number of etchings by Käthe Kollwitz, all condemnatory of war. Nearby is a collection of Oriental porcelains, assembled by the Elector Frederick Augustus I, which helped him introduce the manufacture of fine porcelain into Europe. The museum housing the Royal Treasure contains room after room of furniture and artifacts of fabulous craftsmanship, jewels,

Modern commercial buildings line the Prager Strasse in the heart of the rebuilt city of Dresden.

The vast courtyard of Dresden's renowned Zwinger Palace, a masterpiece of Baroque architecture, which was flattened during the war, has been painstakingly restored.

At Schloss Moritzburg, tourists cross a bridge over a span of water to enter or leave the former royal hunting lodge, now an art gallery.

The ornate Nymphenbad (Nymph Bath) fountain in the Zwinger Palace in Dresden is a popular subject for photographers.

uniforms, glassware and other objects in immense variety. Outside Dresden, one approaches the royal hunting lodge, Schloss Moritzburg, by crossing a mirror-surfaced lake over a causeway, at the end of which stands the lodge (really a small palace), a most inviting prospect.

The Civic Centre is as modern as tomorrow, a vast plaza, bordered by tall hotels, restaurants, pubs and chic shops. Several fountains add charm and sparkle to the scene. Even on cold days the plaza is crowded with people. Like other cities, Dresden is served by tramways, buses and railways, and, on the Elbe River, by river craft that go south to Prague and north to Hamburg and the sea.

Dresden also is a major industrial city, producing electrical equipment, cameras, electronics, ceramics and precision instruments, and is the site of the GDR's principal technical university.

The Meissen Works, near Dresden, has been producing some of the world's most sought-after porcelain since the 17th century. In Meissen, the bells in the cathedral are of porcelain.

23

Fountains play in the Brunenanlagen Square in Karl-Marx-Stadt.

KARL-MARX-STADT

Formerly called Chemnitz, this city of 303,000 is a major industrial hub that produces about 15 per cent of the gross industrial output of the country. In view of this, it is not surprising that the city has one of the country's principal mechanical engineering colleges. The city is beautifully located in the foothills of the Erz-gebirge Mountains, close to the border of Czechoslovakia.

MAGDEBURG

A major industrial city with a population of 273,000, Magdeburg lies in the middle of the most important farming area of the country. The city supplies about 20 per cent of the national heavy industry output, and specializes in chemicals, motor vehicles, construction materials, textiles, rubber, leather and timber products.

Magdeburg also processes and markets agricultural crops, and refines sugar. One of the most important mechanical engineering colleges is located in Magdeburg. As might be expected, the city is also a principal railway junction point for both national and international lines. Tourists are attracted to the city by the many medieval buildings that still stand.

Among the manufactures are many kinds of machinery and machine tools, electrical and electronic products, toys, musical instruments and paper.

From the top of this dam at Magdeburg, children visiting from Poland look a long way down.

After having been totally destroyed, Rostock's Langen Strasse (Long Street) has not only been rebuilt but modernized.

HALLE

Halle, a leading industrial city of 244,000 people, is also a major railway transportation hub, the largest transshipment point in the country. It is the site of the headquarters of Interchim, the socialist-bloc trade organization for the chemical products industries, which promotes international integration, as well as a principal teacher's training college. Halle is the birthplace of the composer, George Frederick Handel.

The principal industries of Halle are chemical production, coal, engineering, locomotives and cars, mining, building materials, and footwear.

ROSTOCK

This old seaport, once a member of the Hanseatic League of North European trading towns, has, with its population of 209,000, taken on new life during the past three decades. Under modern administration, it has grown and developed beyond what it had been before

The central square breaks the monotony of a new satellite town built near booming Rostock.

25

This row of pleasing old buildings has been restored as a reminder to the present generation of Rostock's long past.

Rostock has world-wide ocean and international rail connections and also has road and rail-ferry links with Denmark and Sweden. The port is equipped with the most modern cargo-handling and ship-maintenance facilities. Nuclear power adds to the area's supply of electrical energy. But the past is close at hand. Many buildings have come down from centuries ago, and the University of Rostock, a focal point of research and of advanced studies, dates from 1409.

World War II, during which it was heavily bombed. Not only is it now the principal seaport of the GDR but it has also become important for shipbuilding and as a base for a fishing fleet, and is the chief town of a seaside resort area.

SMALLER CITIES

Half a dozen other important cities have more than 100,000 people each, and no fewer than 136 towns have between 15,000 and 100,000. Clearly, the GDR is a highly urbanized country.

The old and the new are mingled in Erfurt, where some of the buildings date from the 9th century, others from the 20th.

Two years after the end of World War II, the severely damaged tower of Berlin's city hall stood among a sea of gutted buildings.

2. HISTORY

GERMAN HISTORY is now written differently in East and West, reflecting opposing ideologies. In an effort to be objective, the following outline, which may be reasonably acceptable to both sides, is offered as a balance between the two:

EARLY AND MEDIEVAL TIMES

The Germans descend mainly from Teutonic tribes that spread over Europe more than two thousand years ago, mingling their blood with that of various other peoples. For a while the armies of imperial Rome held them in check. When that imperial power declined, Charle-magne, king of the Franks, united what are now France, Germany, the Low Countries and Italy under his rule. In 843, after his death, his empire was broken up, the easternmost part becoming the nucleus of the Holy Roman Empire. Within this loose entity, German kings opened up Central Europe to their emerging culture, defended it against waves of invading barbarians, and eventually brought the Magyars and western Slavs into the fold of their medieval civilization.

Under dukedoms, principalities, petty kingdoms and city-states, feudal society and culture developed, while economic life thrived

After years of neglect, this Benedictine monastery at Paulinzella, near Rudolstadt in the Gera District, has been restored and is now an important tourist attraction.

Wartburg Castle in Erfurt District was important during the Middle Ages. Inside its walls, Luther translated the Bible into German. Later, Goethe sponsored making it into a museum, and Wagner used it as a setting for his singers.

in trading towns, the northernmost of which, grouped in the Hanseatic League, spread their trade throughout much of the known world. In the 15th and 16th centuries, two events took place in Germany that changed Western societies. The invention of printing revolutionized the storing and communication of knowledge, and Martin Luther's split with Roman Catholicism led to Protestantism and the great religious wars of the next two centuries.

RISE OF PRUSSIA

During the 18th and 19th centuries, Germany's notable intellectual and cultural gifts to the world can be indicated by the mention of Goethe, Bach, Brahms, Beethoven, Kant, Hegel, von Humboldt, Engels, Marx, and Wagner, to name but a few. But, while culture

Quedlinburg is a town that tourists love. Except for the automobiles, the central square looks much as it did during medieval times.

The architectural fantasy of this pavilion brightens the grounds of Frederick the Great's palace, Sans Souci, at Potsdam.

flowered, political development lagged, punctuated by occasional revolts of peasants and others against the exploitative feudal system.

Among the various German states, Prussia became dominant during the long reign (1740–1786) of Frederick the Great, who balanced his formidable military prowess with such gentler pursuits as promoting philosophy and the arts. Prussia continued to play an active rôle in European politics throughout the Napoleonic period, and, later, as a member of the Holy Alliance, helped block the spread of representative, democratic and liberal governments, the feasibility of which had been demonstrated to the world by the self-confident American and French Revolutions.

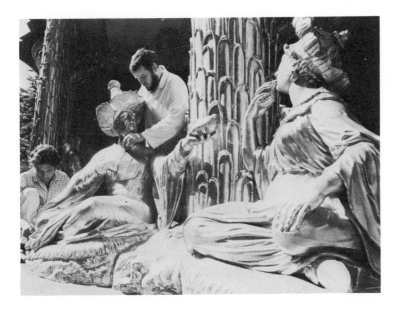

With meticulous, almost loving, care, workers clean and restore sculptures at the Sans Souci palace.

THE COMMUNIST MANIFESTO

During the 19th century, class divisions were widened and sharpened by industrialization, agriculture became commercialized, mining was developed and transportation improved. At the same time several revolutionary political parties appeared on the scene. The publication in 1848 of Karl Marx's and Friedrich Engels' *Communist Manifesto* was a decisive moment in world history. In its time it offered a set of guiding principles to help the working class, wherever found, to achieve the goal of a non-exploitive and classless society. It is still a revolutionary document a century and a quarter later.

Although the German people shared the almost universal urge for modern political institutions, their rulers repressed them until 1848, when revolutionary events in France stimulated German dissatisfaction. An uprising in Berlin wrung from King Friedrich Wilhelm promises of freedom of the press and a constitution. However, a German National Assembly, convened in May, failed to unify the nation, though it approved a Declaration of Fundamental Rights, patterned on the American Declaration of Independence and the French Declaration of the Rights of Man. During the rest of the 19th century, the German people

continued to struggle against exploitation, opposing imperialist war and the enslavement of other peoples, though the odds against them were great.

THE GERMAN EMPIRE

Beginning in 1862, Otto von Bismarck, a reactionary Prussian aristocrat, forged German unity and extended Prussian power through wars with adjacent Denmark, Austria and France. Despite autocratic government, the new German Empire that he created prospered. In Prussia, about 200 families of Junkers, hereditary aristocrats, formed a ruling class. Landless peasants worked the fields, serving 8 or 9 months of the year in the army. Later, the rural workers were fashioned into industrial proletarians, and a capitalist structure of production and distribution became dominant. By the end of the 19th century, Germany had joined other European powers in imperialistic adventures in Asia, Africa and the Pacific.

OVERTHROW OF THE EMPIRE

Emperor Wilhelm II, who came to the throne in 1890, built up Germany's military might, economic strength and political influence. His challenge to the world order represented by Britain, France and Russia, resulted in World War I, the defeat of Germany, economic prostration, social and political disintegration, and the formation of a short-lived liberal democratic government, the Weimar Republic in 1919.

The political gloom represented by Bismarck and Wilhelm II was repeatedly pierced by shafts of light. Millions of Germans could not be denied some acquaintance with liberal political thought. The country that gave the world Marx and Engels also gave Germany a powerful political movement, the Social Democrats. Though this party was unable, for want of free political institutions, to unseat the imperial régime, it had become the strongest single party

Dresden was obliterated toward the close of World War II. This is a view of the blackened, bombed-out heart of the city as late as 1951.

by 1890 and its continued growth through World War I profoundly influenced post-war events.

ADOLF HITLER

Germany's experience of free institutions under the Weimar Republic was short. Until 1924, runaway inflation shattered the economy. For the next five years, government was weak, until, in 1929, hard times and the worldwide depression forced the chief of state, Paul von Hindenburg, to rule arbitrarily. In 1933, Adolf Hitler and his Nazi Party put an abrupt end to Germany's experiment with liberal democracy, and seized power.

During the twilight of the Weimar Republic, the Communist Party grew in strength on the basis of a program for raising the economic level and political power of the working class, opposing the warlike plans of the Nazis, and promoting friendship with the Soviet Union. In 1932, the Communists reached the high point of their influence by promoting a general strike and winning almost 6,000,000 votes, twice that of the Social Democrats at their highest point. They became the chief roadblock to the Nazis in their path to power, and, after Hitler's take-over, were driven underground. They functioned as a resolute home-front resistance organization during the six years of World War II, supported mainly by the Soviet Union.

PARTITION OF GERMANY

Hitler's defeat left Germany again prostrate. Confronted by the threat of famine, epidemics and economic ruin, the victorious wartime allies agreed, at Potsdam in 1945, to demilitarize and decentralize the country. Germany was divided into French, British, United States and Soviet zones. In effect, the country was divided into two unequal parts, the larger Western one under the three Western Allies, the smaller Eastern one under Russia. Berlin, an island in the middle of the eastern section, was likewise divided. The victors also laid on Germany a crushing burden of reparations.

The agreement had hardly been signed before differences arose among the Allies. The Western powers tried to introduce liberal institutions in their occupation zones, while the Soviet Union promoted the acceptance of Marxism-Leninism in theirs. One of the first Russian moves was to fly into East Germany exiled Communist leaders, headed by Walter Ulbricht, who were to organize and build a new nation.

Initially, Soviet policy was harsh. In retaliation for the devastation of the Russian homeland by the Nazis, Soviet troops dismantled factories, tore up railway tracks, and sent East German scientists and technicians to rebuild the Soviet economy instead of their own. The

Seated around this table at Potsdam, the leaders of the victorious Allies mapped out the future of conquered Germany in August, 1945.

Soviets burdened the country with a huge military occupation force, and delayed the restoration of German manpower by forcing German war prisoners to work in Russia.

COMMUNIZATION

The Russian Zone was communized in a relatively short period. Basic industries were confiscated or nationalized, private banks were closed, and all forms of money were seized. But prominent among the drastic actions taken in the Soviet Zone was an agricultural reform scheme that promised immense social and economic gains. Under this project, completed before the middle of 1946, lands that had belonged to some 3,000 landlords were expropriated and distributed among half a million peasants and refugees from former German territories in Eastern Europe.

Within the political structure, German Communists were placed in virtually all key positions. Ulbricht, First Secretary of the Socialist Unity Party (SED), a fusion of the Social Democrats and the Communists, exercised real governmental leadership and power. The SED, it goes without saying, was the heir of the former Communist Party. Other parties, though permitted to function, were formed into a political confederation, known as the Anti-Fascist Bloc of the Democratic Parties, within which they operated as special interest groups, not parties on a plane of equality with the SED. While the SED took their viewpoints into account, it maintained, as the political instrument of the working class, the final power of decision. Three decades later, the lesser political parties appear to accept their secondary political positions in tranquility.

THE GERMAN DEMOCRATIC REPUBLIC

During the summer of 1948, the attempt of the Soviet authorities to drive the Western Allies out of Berlin by closing the surface routes of access to that city was frustrated by a massive U.S. airlift. In 1949, a few months after the Western powers had created the Federal Republic of Germany (West Germany), the Soviets sponsored the founding of the German Democratic Republic, and converted their Military Administration into a Soviet Control Commission. During the next dozen years, approximately 2,700,000 people abandoned the GDR for the West, many of them technically and professionally trained people whom the GDR could ill afford to lose.

Unwilling to see this drain of talent and energy continue, the GDR authorities, in 1961, closed the border and erected the Berlin Wall. Though this drastic act produced an international furor and a still-continuing propaganda storm, it accomplished its purpose. A new phase of development was started. Denied

Onlookers applaud as Otto Grotewohl and Wilhelm Pieck shake hands after uniting the Social Democrats and the Communists in a new Socialist Unity Party (SED), April, 1946.

the easy road of escape, the East Germans accepted dependence on the Soviet Union, and turned their efforts to making the best of their opportunities. The results of their ingenuity and dedicated efforts have been dramatically successful. Before the 1960's had ended, GDR industrial production had increased until it was, in the Communist world, second only to that of the Soviet Union. In the entire world, the GDR was the 9th or 10th most important industrial power by 1977.

Possibly of greater importance, the East Germans have developed a pride in their accomplishments against heavy odds. Today they view their progress with satisfaction, and are eager to show it off to the thousands of foreign visitors who throng their showplaces. In 1976, most of these were from the Federal Republic, many from Eastern Europe, and a growing number from Italy, Spain and France.

October 1961 was a critical period for Berlin and the world, when U.S. and Soviet tanks confronted each other across a street barricade dividing the Allied and Soviet Zones.

THE WALL

The Wall today is hardly a factor, though it is exploited politically by both sides. In the West, it is viewed as making a prison from which the

Berlin, though split, is still nominally under the jurisdiction of the World War II Allies. The U.S. Secretary of State, William Rogers (lower right), signed the 1972 Agreement on West Berlin.

East Germans are desperate to escape; in the East, it is said to be a necessity to protect Socialism's tender shoots from being trampled by imperialism. Neither view has, in 1976, much relationship to the truth. People from West Berlin flock almost without restriction into East Berlin to buy, at the GDR's uninflated prices, books and phonograph records, to visit art galleries and museums and to attend cultural events. Elderly persons are permitted to leave the GDR virtually at will, and younger people have little trouble in obtaining exit permits. If the Wall were removed, it is questionable whether there would be a major population shift in either direction.

But the propaganda value of the Wall is great to both sides. West German officials, on one side of the famous Brandenburg Gate, give their visitors elaborately staged briefings to stress the grim aspects of the barrier. On the other side, GDR officials present equally elaborate briefings to demonstrate the aggressiveness of the West. They offer lectures, exhibits, slide shows and moving pictures detailing the ceaseless harassments and provocations to which their innocent land is subject, including raids into East Berlin by armed gangs, and offensive pornographic displays.

In the light of all this, it is easy to appreciate that a national objective of the GDR is to have

the USSR and the Western Allies agree to the incorporation of East Berlin into the national territory and to have West Berlin recognized as an independent political entity, separate from the Federal Republic.

Thousands of tourists pay their respects to the victims of Nazism at this monument on the site of the infamous Buchenwald concentration camp in the Erfurt District.

In 1972, representatives of the two Germanies signed the Berlin Treaty, which governs the relations between the GDR and West Germany.

3. GOVERNMENT

THE GDR IS A socialist state that is providing rapidly increasing benefits to its population. Neither in an historical nor a geographical sense is it a distinct unit. Its territory did not result from long historical growth; on the contrary, it is no more than that part of the former Germany which Soviet troops, in agreement with the other Allies, occupied at the close of World War II. But it is becoming a nation on the bases of its present geographical area, a homogeneous population, a common language, proud traditions, and now, after more than three decades, general popular acceptance of the socialist order of society and the integration of the nation into the Marxist-Leninist world community.

CONSTITUTION

The basic charter of government is the Constitution, adopted by popular referendum in 1968, which holds the building of an advanced socialist society to be the national goal. While sovereignty is vested in the people, the leading political rôles are reserved for the working class and its Marxist-Leninist party, in alliance with co-operative farmers, the intelligentsia and other progressive elements. It is, its leaders unabashedly concede, a dictatorship of the working class.

The Constitution provides for a socialist reconstruction of society involving such fundamental changes as abolishing the private owner-

The traditional bread and salt are offered in welcome to Erich Honecker, First Secretary of the SED, at a regional festival at Schwerin.

ship of the means of production. This change is counted on to remove exploitation and antagonisms between classes that are, according to socialist doctrine, insurmountable under a capitalist régime. The Constitution includes co-operative farmers within the dominant working class, and accepts as collaborators the progressive intelligentsia, artisans and small tradesmen. The stated over-all objective of the working class is to build a socialist society free of exploitation and oppression.

THE SOCIALIST UNITY PARTY

The principal instrument of the working class in building a new society is, according to the Constitution, the Socialist Unity Party (SED), which mobilizes the working people in pursuit of their own (and therefore the nation's) interest, and formulates policies that, it is said, rest on demonstrable scientific principles.

THE LEGISLATURE

The Constitution establishes the People's Chamber, or national legislature, as the supreme organ of government. In this body, 500 members represent the whole people, but the chamber functions like its counterparts in socialist countries rather than like the legislative bodies of Western democracies. For example,

by design the SED holds more seats than any other party, and controls the functioning of the chamber. The four minor parties and the four mass organizations represented in the chamber are subordinate to the SED, their true function being to communicate views to and from the particular segments of the electorate they represent. Under this arrangement, they are mechanisms through which the formation of a national consensus is facilitated, rather than competitors with different viewpoints.

THE EXECUTIVE

Within the People's Chamber, a 42-member Council of Ministers acts as a cabinet, or administrative organ of government. Over the course of time, this mainly technical body has yielded its powers to 25 of its members, who form a Council of State. Decisions of this Council are legally binding, though subject to ratification by the full People's Chamber. Most members of the Council of State are ranking members of the SED.

THE JUDICIARY BRANCH

The Judiciary is as dependent on the SED as the legislative and executive branches. Judges, elected by representative bodies at several levels, are selected from loyal party members. Doctrine holds that law and justice are, like

In Berlin, an eternal flame burns in this Memorial to the Victims of Fascism and Militarism, to which local people and tourists make pilgrimages.

everything else, tools for the construction of the socialist society. Consequently, the judicial system is an agency through which official doctrine is expressed, and the professional status of a judge depends on both his legal competence and his performance, as evaluated politically by the government and the SED.

The penal code is closely compatible with that of the Soviet Union, though it embodies traditional German law as well. Most sections deal with offenses against the socialist system of government and society; but others define offenses against the régime, the individual, private property, socialist property, public order, and the military structure. The code is administered by a system of courts—one in each district plus more numerous county courts, all under the Supreme Court in Berlin. Each court is divided into a civil and a criminal chamber. Of growing importance in the legal system are the social courts, which were originally set up to deal with labor problems and other close-to-home matters, but which have been taking over more and more minor criminal cases.

The GDR takes pride in the decline of crime to one-fourth of what it had been during the early post-War period. It attributes this in large part to the reduced incentive for crime in a socialist society. There were about 30,000 prison inmates in 1964. In their treatment of prisoners, the government lays stress on rehabilitation programs: job training, paid work projects, and participation in sports.

POLITICAL SUBDIVISIONS

The territory of the GDR is divided for administrative purposes into 14 districts, 217 counties and 9,010 communities. These do not include Berlin (East Germans refer to their part of the city as Berlin, the other part as West Berlin), which, because of its nominal status under four-power occupation, is not formally incorporated within the country. But in practice, it is the undisputed capital.

The districts serve only administrative purposes; their boundaries form no barrier to the movement of people and goods. They are roughly all the same in size and population, subdivided into about 15 counties each, the sizes of which vary considerably.

Until 1952, the divisions of the national territory had been in the form of five provinces —Brandenburg, Mecklenburg, Saxony, Saxony-Anhalt, and Thuringia. These names persist as designations of the general areas in which districts and communities are located, and for this reason are included in the map on page 4, along with other traditional regional names.

THE CIVIL SERVICE

The civil service is controlled by the SED at all levels. In evaluations of employees' performances, political reliability is given weight in addition to technical competence.

Public officials other than the civil service are elected, the suffrage being universal for all over 18. But since the National Front organizes

The First Secretary of the SED has pleasant words for the staff of "Ferdinandshof," a state-owned beef feeding station in Neubrandenburg District. Note silos in the background.

the elections and screens the candidates, voters are limited (except for a write-in vote) to voting for or against candidates nominated for each post by the Front.

POLITICAL PARTIES

The rôle and functions of political parties differ from those of parties in the Western democracies. In the GDR, the SED takes precedence over the state itself, regarding the state as an instrument for promoting and achieving party goals. All government activities are carried out in the name of the working class, and the head of the party is also the head of the Council of State. Within the SED, power is controlled by a Political Bureau, headed by the party's First Secretary.

Each of the four minor parties follows SED leadership, though its base of support is different. The Christian Democratic Union and the Liberal Democratic Party are nominally like their counterparts in the Federal Republic of Germany. The Democratic Peasants' Party and the National Democratic Party were both established by the SED after World War II, the former to organize rural farmers, the latter to appeal to people who had been drawn into the Nazi Party of Hitler's day.

MASS ORGANIZATIONS

Part of the apparatus consists of four mass organizations, each of which mobilizes support from certain population groups. Of these, the largest is the Free German Trade Union Federation, with nearly 7,000,000 members. Next is the Democratic Women's Federation, whose 3,000,000 members promote women's rights, followed by the Free German Youth, with more than 2,000,000 members. Finally, the German Cultural League, ostensibly a non-partisan group of intellectuals, propagates official cultural policies, promoting "creative work according to the creative method of socialist realism." The League has about 110,000 members.

THE NATIONAL FRONT

The minority parties and the mass organizations are joined with the SED in the National Front, which coordinates party and mass-organization policies, allots seats in the People's Chamber and compiles the lists of candidates for elective office. In practice, this organization functions smoothly. Constituent organizations have opportunity to present and promote their viewpoints and defend their interests. The SED

Folk dancers from Soviet Tadzhikistan entertain at tea time in the House of GDR-USSR Friendship, Berlin.

apparently takes the different views seriously and tries to accommodate them within the national decisions. The conduct and purpose of the SED seem well-intentioned, and the directing officials of the Front without apology acknowledge that the Front is a principal mechanism through which the working class and its party, the SED, exercise their dictatorship, and make it palatable to other political groups.

PUBLIC ORDER AND SECURITY

In a country traditionally known for its love of order and disposition to obey authority, the organizational structure to maintain security is varied. The Ministry of the Interior administers the People's Police, which ensures public order and security, protects the socialist state, fights fires, controls traffic, and prevents and controls crime.

Among the most important internal and external security forces is the Workers' Militia, a paramilitary group numbering more than 370,000 men, ranging from 25 to 60 in age. Women have been regular members of militia units, though their participation has become less prominent than it was during the 1950's and 1960's.

Civil Defense Forces, spread nation-wide, protect people and places against air attack, fight fires, and help preserve order. Specialized units provide medical and veterinary services, perform tasks of salvage and construction,

help provide transport and meteorological services. Since 1970, they have been charged with responding to natural catastrophes.

ALERT UNITS

Alert Units are elite military units, which in 1971 numbered about 10,000 men. More heavily armed than the police or militia, they perform internal security functions. Recruits are likely to come from the Free German Youth, and their training is political as well as military.

The Ministry for State Security is an active and militant organ of government power, dedicated to oppose—with the assistance of the Soviet Union—espionage, sabotage, economic disturbances, ideological deviation, provocations, and "other machinations of Western imperialism." The Ministry collects foreign intelligence, and is presumed to have internal security functions as well, especially in counteracting Western intelligence operations.

Government security agencies try to enlist the voluntary co-operation of the people. Examples are paramilitary groups that have twice as many members as regular military units, and youth and labor organizations with their large memberships.

Among the surveillance measures are requirements that people carry identification cards with photograph, address, and other detail, and that in addition workers carry certificates with full employment records. Since 1970, documentary controls have been increased. A large variety of personal and other information is coded on identification cards and birth

A young marksman takes careful aim at the Spartakiad Games Olympic-style competitions.

certificates, and is used in wage and salary accounting, social security records, insurance and pension data, business transactions, bank accounts, school records, travel data, medical treatment and history, etc. These details are deposited in computer banks for ready reference.

MILITARY SYSTEM

The GDR's military forces are strong, well equipped and highly trained. In 1971, about 6 per cent of men of military age were in active service, and an equal number in trained reserves. The National People's Army, comprised of ground, air and sea forces, is under the tight control of the SED, actually under the personal control of the First Secretary of the party, and plays a full part in the military activities of the Warsaw Pact, which is the Communist counterpart of NATO.

Overshadowing national armed forces in strength are the elite military units of the Soviet Union that are stationed on East German soil, to balance NATO forces in the West.

The Houses of Young Pioneers offer a variety of crafts, sports and other occupations to teen-agers. This one is at Schwerin.

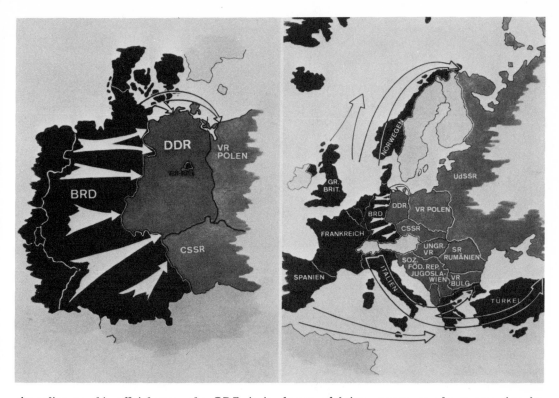

According to this official map, the GDR is in danger of being overrun at almost any time by enveloping NATO forces. BRD, at left, are the German initials of the Federal Republic of Germany (West Germany). CSSR stands for Czechoslovakia.

FOREIGN RELATIONS

Since its founding in 1949, the GDR has pursued two main foreign policy objectives—getting its boundaries established and obtaining recognition of its independence by the community of nations. The break-through in obtaining recognition came in 1969, when a number of the non-aligned nations recognized it. Today, the United States and most major countries have diplomatic relations with the GDR, which is also a member of the United Nations. The 1975 Helsinki Agreement put a seal of international acceptance on the territorial boundaries.

Political, economic and military relationships with the Soviet Union take precedence over all others, and are closely intertwined. Distinct from the formal government-to-government relations is the more important power relationship between the SED and the Communist Party of the USSR. In addition, many other points of contact support the overall relationship, such as the Society for German-Soviet Friendship, trade union federations, official youth and other organizations, and the consultative relations existing between several of the government ministries with their Soviet counterparts. There are even factory-to-factory and school-to-school relationships. The Warsaw Pact and other agreements are the framework for GDR relationships with socialist countries.

GDR foreign policy supports the general principle of aiding "peoples' aspirations for freedom and independence," and such other principles as the SED may elucidate and approve. The First Secretary of the SED has an undisputed rôle of foreign policy leadership.

Young people enjoy dancing at the Zapust, an ethnic festival of the Sorb minority, held at the end of February in the Cottbus District.

Leipzigers are likely to be found around the Sachsenplatz (Saxony Square), strolling or sipping drinks during the summer afternoons.

The revolutionary implications of the old Roman play, "Spartacus," are appreciated by the audience at this forest amphitheatre at Thale.

In Leipzig, the widely acclaimed Thomaner Choir, composed of boys from 10 to 18, specializes in Bach chorales.

4. THE PEOPLE

THE ETHNICALLY AND culturally homogeneous East Germans include the Germanic Prussians, Saxons and Thuringians, with a small minority of Slavic Sorbs living in a region historically known as Lusatia, southeast of Berlin. The Sorbs (also called Wends) are encouraged to preserve their culture, schools, publications and language (which is akin to Polish and Czech). Germans of East and West speak the same standard German (though local dialects persist) and have a similar cultural background. But divided politically, as they have been since the end of World War II, they are drifting apart.

Hardly a vestige of the pre-war feudal class structure remains. The old landed aristocracy has been dispossessed and, with the nationalization of industry and trade, affluent commoners have been submerged also. A small remnant of the former middle class survives in the tiny private sector of the economy. Soviet policy has fostered these changes.

POPULATION

The GDR has a population estimated in 1976 at 16,900,000. Imbalance in the population structure—that is, 9,100,000 females as against 7,800,000 males—is a matter of official concern, but the fact that males outnumber females in the 6–15 age group suggests that the balance is being redressed. Birth and death rates were 10.6 and 13 per thousand in 1974, leaving a net decline rate of 2.4 per thousand. This decline has implications on national power, food supply and standard of living. From 18,300,000 in 1950, the population has dropped to an estimated 16.9 million in 1976. The work force of about 10,000,000, equally divided between the sexes, comprises over half the total population. Retired persons, two-thirds of them women, comprise a disproportionate one fifth of the population.

Generally, the areas of heaviest settlement are

Despite official indifference, religion is an important element in GDR life. As shown, St. Hedwig's Cathedral continues to draw worshippers in Berlin.

It is the official view that the humanistic aims of socialism are compatible with Christianity, a view that seems shared by churchmen. Government relations with the various religious institutions are the province of a State Secretariat for Church Affairs, and some religious leaders have said that their communities probably enjoy about as much freedom as "they can use."

The country has a larger Protestant population than any other socialist country in Eastern Europe. About 8 per cent of the people profess Roman Catholicism. Among the Protestants, the Lutheran and Reformed Churches, the strongest denominations, are united in a Federation of Protestant Churches. Methodists, Baptists and various Pentecostal sects are lesser

along the Baltic coast, the banks of the Oder River, and west of Berlin. Approximately 57 per cent of the population is found in the central lowlands, where the highest density is west of Berlin. With the exception of Rostock, all the most important cities are located south of Berlin. About 26 per cent of the people live in rural areas, more than 45 per cent in cities of 20,000 or more. In recent years, the industrialization of the southern and southwestern upland regions has led to sharp population growth there.

RELIGION

The GDR government, like that of the United States, neither promotes nor hinders religious practice. There is no established church, and, under the constitution, the freedoms of belief and expression are recognized.

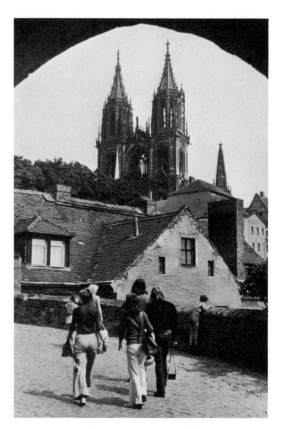

The towers of the Gothic cathedral at Meissen, near Dresden, look over the city, which has been famed for porcelain since the 17th century.

Old customs persist. Here a bride wears the traditional white veil as she signs the marriage register. GDR authorities boast that under socialism young couples are free from worries for their economic future.

groups. Of the once prosperous Jewish community, which numbered close to 200,000 before the rise of Hitler, only 750 remained in 1977.

Churches own property, operate hospitals, nursing homes, children's homes and homes for the aged. Clergymen are trained at the universities, where, like other students, they receive government grants. The government pays clergymen's salaries and old-age pensions, in addition to financing the preservation of church buildings and art works.

The strength of religious feeling among the people makes it politic for the government to co-exist with the churches, but in a relationship that is neither equal nor easy. The government alone is permitted to propagate its views throughout the entire society. While Marxists believe that religion will wither away with the spread of education and the passage of the generations, the church has not died, though the practice of religion is changing. Worship is tending to move out of public places and into private homes, while formal public rituals are yielding place to informal discussions and small study and worship groups.

THE ARTS AND CULTURE

Marxist doctrine gives the arts and culture an important rôle. First, they are not to be exploited for private gain, and second, they must be brought within reach of the people. Third, they are fostered for the contribution they can make to the development of socialism.

Art and cultural institutions—libraries, publishing houses, theatres and record companies—are under public control. Doctrine further holds that, for the progress of society, the working class should be the source of inspiration and provide the subjects for new works of art. It is not strange, then, that government expenditures on cultural projects have more than doubled each ten years since 1952.

Visitors could spend many hours looking at the art treasures on display at the Baudenkmäler und Kuntswerke, in Potsdam.

Dinosaur skeletons attract interest in the Berlin Natural History Museum.

MUSEUMS

Government support of culture and art is evident in the number of museums and art galleries. There are 17 major museums, one in each leading city plus others in secondary cities. Specialized museums include 13 devoted to literary and cultural history, 12 technical museums, 10 of ethnology, 7 of history, 7 combining several specialities, and 6 of natural science.

Among the leading museums is the Pergamon Museum in Berlin, which houses world-renowned collections of art, sculpture and artifacts from classic times to the present, including the famous bust of Egypt's Queen Nefertiti. Also in Berlin is the Museum of German History, where, besides its regular exhibits, special exhibits—for example, graphic arts—are offered. The People's Palace in Berlin is also a gallery, where many large canvases are on display, most of them contemporary and on revolutionary themes.

TRAINING AND PROMOTION

Most cities have art galleries, concert halls, and theatres, while government promotion of all forms of cultural expression reaches down to village and neighborhood levels. A principal agency serving a promotional purpose is the House of Young Talent, an organization devoted to finding and developing talent of all kinds. On any given day in the Berlin central headquarters, for example, individual and group training is offered in many fields—ballet, folk and exhibition dancing, gymnastics, dramatics, poetry and creative writing, journalism, instrumental and vocal music, public speaking, and television programming, to name some. No matter what the talent, the government provides the best available instruction and training. With such help at hand for the asking, East German creative expression is expanding.

Artistic expression is also encouraged and supported through schools, trade unions, children's and youth organizations. There are

Gret Palucca, renowned ballerina, teaches in the State Ballet School, Berlin.

approximately 1,000 culture clubs and nearly as many interest and study groups. Music is given special emphasis, as might be expected in a country that has given the world Bach, Schumann and Handel. In every village and neighborhood there is likely to be, besides an oompah brass band, a choir, glee club, and string ensemble.

As participation in cultural activities has spread through the population, government investment has increased; and artists of all kinds, because of their mass audiences, can exert their influence on society.

FESTIVALS

In addition to the usual holidays and festivals, the government stresses those which can be said to be traditionally German. Christmas, for example, is celebrated with great joy. Weeks prior to the date, Christmas decorations are seen everywhere, and kiosks are set up on city streets to sell ornaments and gifts. Holidays associated with working class history are officially promoted.

The largest public celebration is the annual Berlin Festival in October. It is a week-long gala with broad international participation celebrating the anniversary of the founding of the GDR.

There are many cultural festivals. The Biennial Music Festival stresses contemporary music, the Berlin Festival of Political Song attracts entrants from many countries, and musical contests in Zwickau, Leipzig and Halle honor Schumann, Bach and Handel, respectively.

Some of the world's finest musical instruments have traditionally been manufactured in Germany. This GDR craftsman is making a clarinet key.

A tipsy Bacchus adorns a float at a traditional Winterfest at Freyburg, in the Halle District.

The International Documentary Short Film Week in Leipzig has worldwide prestige.

There are many smaller festivals in villages, boroughs, factories, neighborhoods and schools, some of which have come down through long tradition and have been adapted to serve socialist cultural purposes.

FOOD

One of the first impressions a visitor to the GDR receives is the quantity of food consumed. From breakfast through lunch, afternoon tea, and dinner, meals are huge and, by Western standards, heavy. The principal restaurants offer international cuisines, though those of socialist countries predominate. German foods are the most widely consumed fare, and the absence of French names from menus is noticeable. Venison, wild boar, and wild fowl appear commonly on menus. In addition to regular restaurants, there are many smaller eating places and numerous snack stands, lunch counters, and ice cream stands. The quality of food is generally from adequate to high. Beer is the almost universal beverage, though soft drinks are widely available. Wine is generally offered, and there is no lack of hard liquors.

Supermarkets and other food stores are amply stocked with worldwide varieties of produce, tropical as well as temperate. Milk, butter and many kinds of cheese are abundant. Meat

Residents enjoy beer and dancing at a garden party in the Weidenweg Home for the Aged, Berlin.

This centuries-old Berlin restaurant takes its name, "The Last Resort," from the custom of participants in legal proceedings to repair there for a drink after the proceedings are finished.

counters offer a full range of cuts of beef, lamb, pork and poultry, while seafood sections are stocked with ocean fish, lobsters and shellfish, and such fresh-water fish as carp and trout. An amazing variety of sausages and cold-cuts is on display, the most sought-after coming from Thuringia.

Restaurants are well patronized, as most people can apparently afford to eat out, at least occasionally. Having Sunday dinner at a restaurant seems to be the custom of a great many families, either after church or a visit to the park or zoo. For tourists, it is pleasant to see parents and grandparents and possibly uncles and aunts at public tables, accompanied by lively and well-mannered children.

Berliners enjoy a snack at a half open-air restaurant typical of the nearby Spreewald recreation area.

This young woman participant in a Berlin competition clears the high-jump bar at 6 feet 3 inches (1.88 metres) but with little to spare.

Cyclists whiz around the stadium in a Berlin competition.

Boys and girls from Cottbus and its suburbs are taught to swim in a pool maintained by a local chemical factory.

Grace and elegance are the goals of these women gymnasts, whose sport is growing very rapidly in the GDR.

SPORTS

Wherever they go in the GDR, travellers are likely to be impressed by the number, size and equipment of public sports facilities. Sports grounds, playing fields, gymnasiums, indoor and outdoor swimming pools abound. If they relate this to the success of GDR athletes, they will appreciate the degree to which the government supports athletics.

Foremost among the organizations used for this purpose is the German Gymnastics and Sports Federation, a mass organization that promotes both leisure-time and high-performance sports, in close cooperation with the German Youth Organization, the Ministry of Education, and representative organizations. One of its missions is to encourage international sports as a contribution to the relaxation of international tensions and to the peaceful co-existence of states with different social systems.

Sports are officially regarded as an important political activity. The 1968 constitution provides for the participation in sports as a personal right supportive of the physical and mental development of the citizens. While sports are not directly professionalized, as Western critics often allege, probably nothing is left un-

done to enable promising competitors to develop prowess and participate in international competitions.

In 1974, there were active associations for soccer, gymnastics, swimming, skiing, track and field, boxing, cycling, riding, bowling, angling, handball, volleyball, ping-pong, judo,

The marathon run is for young and old. In this photo, the youngster is 10, his grandfather, 69.

Modern techniques are used in this school for rehabilitating handicapped children, in the Erfurt District.

chess, motoring, tennis, mountaineering, riding, canoeing, and yachting. These associations had more than 2.5 million members.

Probably no one in the population is far removed from sports facilities. Individual participants and teams are found not only in schools but also in industrial, agricultural and commercial work groups, local communities, and trade unions. It would seem to require effort to avoid being drawn into sports.

Participation begins at an early age. Children take part in annual Spartakiad Games, in which competitions in most Olympic events are held at schools and in other localities. In recent years, more than 12,000 youngsters have entered summer events, and 1,300 winter events, out of which many of the country's sports stars have come.

The GDR is a member of 79 European and international sports organizations, and regards its 1966 agreement on sports with the USSR as a mainstay of its close relationship with the Soviet Union. Popular pride in the success of national teams is great. A soccer victory over another country, for example, is almost certain to lead to dancing in the streets.

EDUCATION

The elaborate educational structure rests squarely on the idea that real education is possible only in societies in which the means of production are collectively owned, the relations of people and institutions involved in the production process are harmonious, and the exploitation of man by man has been eliminated. Leaders of the GDR believe these conditions have been achieved.

They believe that education is political in the sense of supporting the struggle of the working class and embracing a "scientific, Marxist-

Television is used for instruction at Friedrich Schiller University, Jena.

Workers in an electrical factory sort through books offered by the factory's mobile library.

Leninist outlook upon nature and society." They stress that education is the same for all, without distinction between popular and élite schooling, and a child's career is not predetermined by the education received. Since the Soviet Union is regarded as the leader of the socialist world, Russian is taught as the first foreign language at all educational levels.

Infant care facilities and kindergartens have multiplied greatly since 1950; but the basis of the educational system is the co-educational Ten-Grade Polytechnic School, which consists of three levels. Grades 1–3 study reading, writing and arithmetic, complemented by studies of socialist society and elementary work experience in methods of socialist production. Grades 4–6 prepare for specialized studies, and 7–10 receive specialized instruction.

At all levels, instruction is provided in manual skills—carpentry, metal working, plastics moulding and farming. From the seventh grade on, students are trained directly in industrial plants. Of the graduates of these schools, 90 per cent go on to learn a trade in two-year apprenticeships in socialist enterprises, and the best are given a chance to join research teams in

Tots wash up at a day-care facility in Leipzig. In 1976, there were day-care places for 484 out of every 1,000 children in the proper age group.

Residents in Homes for the Aged are kept in contact with the life surrounding them. This resident is telling stories to children from a nearby school.

industrial organizations. Special schools are provided for gifted students, of which the most qualified are selected for university education. Practical on-the-job work training is continued at all levels.

The GDR has general universities at Berlin, Leipzig, Halle, Jena, Rostock and Greifswald; a University of Technology and a Military Academy at Dresden. Since 1945, nearly 200 technical schools have been established. Capping the educational system are research institutes—the Academy of Sciences and the Academy of Agricultural Sciences in Berlin, the Saxon Academy of Sciences at Leipzig, and the Leopoldina Academy of Natural Science at Halle.

Adult education is offered in factories and village educational centers. Adult educational institutes expand popular knowledge, and universities and technical schools offer continuing education for their graduates.

An unusual feature of rearing the young is the *Jugendweihe*, a ceremony whereby children, on reaching 14, are symbolically admitted to the adult world. Boys and girls are prepared in special classes for life in the socialist community, taught about German progressive traditions, and indoctrinated in the revolutionary struggle of the German and international working class. This has the earmarks of a throw-back to the pagan puberty rites of prehistoric Teutonic tribes.

Teacher training is provided at universities and normal schools. Teachers, who are organized into a professional trade union, enjoy positions of respect, and are honored especially on an annual Teachers' Day.

PUBLIC INFORMATION

The government controls all public information media through various levels of the SED party apparatus. The government owns radio and television facilities, book publishing houses, the sole news agency, and, in addition, controls the allocation of newsprint. The SED Politburo issues guidelines for editorials and articles, and exercises an almost total supervision. Its purposes are to promote the domestic and foreign objectives of the SED, and disseminate information designed to broaden mass support.

In 1971, the newspapers included 38 dailies, about 30 weeklies, and some 600 factory house organs. The nine dailies published in East Berlin have the greatest prestige and nationwide circulations. The most important, *Neues Deutschland*, founded in 1945, is the semi-official voice of the government. Other Berlin papers are the morning *Berliner Zeitung* and the evening *Berliner Zeitung am Abend*. Statistics show that 515 magazines and periodicals were being published in 1974, but fewer than four dozen are widely known throughout the country. The official German

Two movie actors make an attractive pair filming a 1973 DEFA-Farbfilm production.

News Service (ADN) has many offices abroad. It is the only news agency.

Book publishing is a function of the Ministry of Culture, to which private publishers must submit their plans. While Leipzig, "Book City," has been the traditional publishing capital, Berlin now ranks higher. In 1974, 5,697 new books and pamphlets were printed, with a total run of 127,218,000 copies. Of these, 861 were translations of foreign works, of which many are of United States authors. International trade in books and publications is controlled by an official agency.

Electronic media are well developed. The State Committee for Radio operates 33 radio and 17 television stations. In 1974, radio receivers licensed numbered 6,113,600 and televisions, 5,095,700. This means that practically every household in the country has radio and nearly every household television as well.

The Ministry of Culture supervises and controls all motion picture film production, and the German Film Company handles all export and import of films. In 1974, there were 831 moving picture theatres in operation, about half the number of two decades ago.

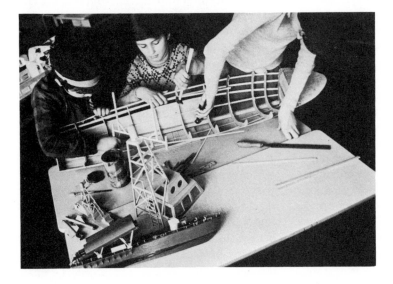

Building ship models develops craft skills in GDR's schools, like this one in Karl-Marx-Stadt.

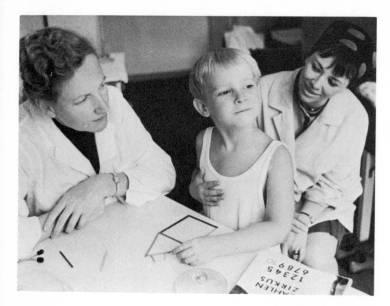

A pre-schooler is given a medical examination prior to entering elementary school.

HEALTH

Free medical care is provided to everyone in the GDR, without regard to social position or place of residence. All health services are under government control and aim to make modern medicine accessible to all citizens, raise the quality of diagnostic, preventive and curative services, and deepen the confidence among citizens, health personnel and health institutions.

Immunization against communicable diseases is compulsory. Polio has been wiped out, diphtheria is extremely rare, measles is no longer widespread, and tuberculosis has ceased to be a scourge.

The GDR gives high priority to the care of the elderly. Those in the picture are combining exercise with fun in a game of tug-of-war. Those who can afford to pay are charged DM 2.50 ($1) per day in Homes for the Aged—others are taken care of free.

Large potash works at Preseteritz, Halle District, are among the most modern in Europe, and help support the important chemical industry.

5. THE ECONOMY

THE GDR IS a component of the socialist world, linked by an intricate web of interrelationships. Overall planning is integrated with the plans of the USSR and other socialist nations, and economic production similarly dovetailed with the output of Warsaw Pact allies. It follows that foreign trade is mainly with the USSR and the socialist world. For example, in 1974, 90 per cent of imports and exports went to and came from socialist countries, about a third of the total to and from the Soviet Union. Most of the rest of the trade was with industrial capitalist countries. The total volume of foreign trade nearly tripled between 1965 and 1976.

An intelligent and industrious citizenry who are masters of sophisticated skills and highly advanced technology, have transformed the GDR from a mainly food-producing area of primitive agricultural structure to the most highly industrialized and affluent country in the socialist world, on the verge of becoming a high-consumption economy. Since 1949 planned economic goals have been regularly exceeded and an economic miracle wrought.

WORK FORCE

Since 1965, the number of employed workers has risen from 7,700,000 to 7,900,000, about equally divided between the sexes, and all organized within official trade unions. There is no unemployment. Indeed, authorities try to cope with a chronic manpower shortage in many

In the northern city of Schwerin, modern apartments have been built to house 60,000 people since the end of World War II.

ways. For example, public eating places are often self-service buffet style, as often as not no one collects tickets on streetcars and buses (though riders scrupulously buy them), and service personnel of all kinds is scarce. Automobile motors have been changed from 4-cycle to 2-cycle because the latter use fewer parts and require less effort to build and maintain. Also, the traveller's attention is drawn to the sight of U.S.-built power mowers on East German lawns and parks swept by U.S.-made vacuum cleaners.

COST OF LIVING

Price levels have remained relatively stable. Committees on which consumers, trade unions, producers and government are represented fix

In Karl-Marx-Stadt, a worker and his young family move into a new apartment.

Families flock to the Warnemünde beaches, where the fine white sand can be moulded into castles defended by toy soldiers.

the prices of foods, rents and manufactured goods on a variety of bases, of which cost of production seems to be given less weight than others. The principle is that necessities should be priced low and luxuries high, and that proceeds from the high prices should be used to subsidize the lower ones. Once fixed, prices tend to remain in effect indefinitely; most prices today were fixed during the 1960's, some even earlier.

PRIORITIES

Strange to Western concepts, socialist enterprise in the GDR seems to have priorities unlike those in capitalist countries. The most important purpose of an industry appears to be to provide economic, educational, cultural and recreational benefits to its workers. The second is to provide revenue for the government. The last is to produce goods. These priorities are possible in a non-competitive, socialist economy, where industries have no domestic competition.

A notable feature of the socialist economy is the absence of competition, not only among industries and business establishments but among individuals as well. Major industries and businesses are monopolies, with their non-competitive positions assured by law or regulation. This is bound to result in lessened efficiency of production. Less measurable is the effect of economic non-competition among the people. A society that offers cradle-to-the-grave security minimizes an individual's urge to struggle to get ahead.

There are specific signs that the system is not flawless. In contrast to socialist ideals, the custom of tipping persists—for taxi drivers, hotel maids, pages and cloakroom attendants, waiters, and barbers. The reason usually given for this is that persons performing such services, while they are assured a decent wage, may

receive at least as much and more in gratuities. In other words, a capitalist kind of incentive attracts those willing to accept menial positions.

AGRICULTURE

A traveller is likely to be impressed by the huge farms and few farmers of the countryside, and by the massive degree of farm mechanization. This is a development of recent years and is a major change from pre-war times, when the land was divided into large, absentee-owned and peasant-farmed estates of low productivity. The changes brought by the socialist restructuring of the country put an end to this system. Since 1952, when co-operative farming was introduced, virtually all of the land has come under collective ownership, and a country that formerly had to import food is now a net exporter.

Comparable changes have been made in the cultivation pattern. The relative increase in the growing of feed crops reflects an upgrading of the national diet toward higher protein levels.

Co-operative farming makes possible a high degree of mechanization. In this photo a "Brigade of Ten" harvesters moves across a broad field.

Large-scale agriculture makes possible improved conditions of life and culture for the rural population. Their standard of living and opportunities for cultural uplifting are now about the same as those available to urban workers. In addition, educational and health services have been made available to the farm population. Such changes lie behind the great increase in agricultural productivity. The success of collective and co-operative farms explains a change in farmers' attitudes—today they think of socially owned farms as giving them an ownership stake, instead of being the property of some far-off, seldom-seen proprietor. The new generation of rural dwellers which has emerged frankly accepts the Marxist tenet that the means of production should be nationally owned.

The leading crops are potatoes, sugar beets, wheat, rye, barley, oats and hay. Cattle, sheep, pigs and poultry are the chief animals raised.

FISHERIES

Ocean and freshwater fisheries have been greatly expanded. In 1956, deep-sea fishing produced 62,200 metric tons, and inland fisheries, 6,400 tons. In 1974, these figures had risen to 312,000 and 13,400 tons, respectively.

An autumn scene in the Spreewald Forest in the Cottbus District. Melons lie among the autumn leaves at the starting point for boating parties.

A prize Charolais bull is paraded before an appreciative audience at an agricultural fair at Markleeburg, in Leipzig District.

GAME

Through scientific management and conservation practices, wild game has been made into a renewable resource, an important contribution to the food and fur supply as well as offering popular sport and recreation. Deer, hares, wild boars, wild ducks and geese are plentiful and increasing in numbers. Fur-bearing animals trapped are foxes, martens and ermines.

FOREST PRODUCTS

Forests are under scientific management. In 1974 they yielded 7,100 cubic metres of timber, approximately half of it in saw logs. This was an increase of more than 25 per cent over that of 1965.

INDUSTRY

The strongest industries are chemicals and precision engineering, many of which have been integrated with the economies of adjacent socialist countries. Industrial development has proceeded in accordance with successive national development plans, which have been coordinated as far as possible with those of adjacent socialist countries in order to bring about a significant international specialization of production.

Industrialization has been achieved at high cost owing to the obstacles posed by, for example, the dependence on lignite as a fuel and source of crude chemicals. But blast furnaces are fed by lignite-based coke, and the production of iron and steel has been expanded in compensation for the loss of normal pre-war supplies from the Federal Republic of Germany. Today, GDR industry is heavily dependent on iron ore from the Soviet Ukraine, and fuel from Poland and the USSR, including petroleum pipelined from the distant Caucasus and Urals.

In this modern cattle farm shed in Neubrandenburg District, 8,500 yearlings can be fed at one time.

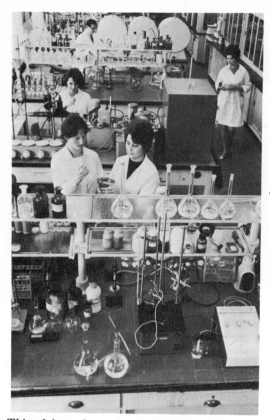

This elaborately equipped laboratory in Karl-Marx-Stadt helps develop and improve the synthetic fibres used in the textile industry.

Skills for high-precision manufacturing are abundant in the GDR. These Dresden women are assembling fine cameras.

TRANSPORTATION

Land, water and air transportation are highly developed and have grown greatly since 1960. Railways are the most important, followed closely by river and canal traffic. The partition of the country has changed the predominant traffic flow from east and west to north and south.

The various forms of surface transportation provide easy circulation for both people and goods, since natural land features offer only minor obstacles. Railways provide fast and frequent service throughout the country, motor roads criss-cross the entire area, and few places are remote from internal waterways. The state-owned airline, *Interflug*, flies both internal and international routes, mostly to eastern Europe. All surface and air transportation is linked to contiguous countries and, by ferry, to Sweden, Norway and Denmark. Long-distance air service is offered to Helsinki, Hanoi and Havana, and to Cairo, Conakry (Guinea) and Khartoum (Sudan). The principal trans-Eurasian stop is Moscow, but routes continue to Delhi and Dacca (Bangladesh), and to Tashkent (in Soviet Central Asia) and Kandahar (Afghanistan).

There has been little change in the lengths of internal road, railway and waterway routes, but the volumes of cargoes hauled over each have gone up nearly five times since 1949.

OUTLOOK FOR THE FUTURE

The GDR will in all likelihood continue to prosper and develop during the coming years, within an increasingly intricate web of inter-

A vigorous import and export trade has made Rostock a world port, equipped with the most modern cargo handling machinery, and always crowded with shipping.

relationships with the socialist community of nations, and separate and distinct from the adjacent Federal Republic. The higher living standards in the GDR as compared to its socialist partners, already evident, will continue. But there is no reason to expect any basic change in its ideological orientation toward socialism.

As history unfolds and détente grows more robust, GDR ties with the West should develop more closely and on more levels of contact. This in itself should have a softening influence on life within the GDR society, especially as the generations of East Germans to come are likely to be more open to the values and influences of other cultures.

INDEX